CATS

RE:BOOKS

www.rebooks.ca

Published in Canada by RE:BOOKS

RE:BOOKS
Brookfield Place
181 Bay Street
Toronto, Ontario
M5J 2T9
Canada

www.rebooks.ca

First RE:BOOKS Edition: December 2023

ISBN: 978-1-7389452-8-3
eBook ISBN: 978-1-7389452-9-0

RE:BOOKS and all associated logos are trademarks and/or registered marks of RE:BOOKS.

Printed and bound in Canada.
1 3 5 7 9 10 8 6 4 2

Cover Design By: Emilee Corey and Jordan Lunn
Typeset By: Karl Hunt

CATS

Pamela Wallin

Kitty

Dedication

This book is dedicated to ailurophiles —
who love and understand the mind and
spirit of the cat.

And also to Kitty,
who will always be a part of me.

There are two means of refuge
from the miseries of life:
music and the cat.

–ALBERT SCHWEITZER

Contents

"Of all God's creatures,
there is only one that cannot be made the
slave of the leash. That one is the cat.
If man could be crossed with the
cat it would improve man,
but it would deteriorate the cat."

–MARK TWAIN

Introduction

CATS are not perfect. They can be a little demanding and to risk understatement, very self-centered. But they are also extraordinary, loyal creatures, and once you have won their affection, the comfort they offer their human companions is like no other. It is true that the love and affection a dog will give you is more physical and enthusiastic. Author Mary Bly once said, "Dogs come when they're called; cats take a message and get back to you later." A dog loves unconditionally, and is openly grateful for the simplest kindness. A cat, however, need not apologize for being conditional. As the French poet and painter Théophile Gautier wrote, "It is difficult to win the friendship of a cat. It is a philosophical animal—one that does not place its affections thoughtlessly."

Cats are emotionally disciplined. They do not hesitate to withhold affection as a behaviour modification technique—even as punishment—and they demand a lot more control in a relationship. As any cat owner knows, "cat owner" is a contradiction in terms. Cats are individuals who insist on their right to make their own decisions. Their proud confidence both demands and commands respect.

Cats can recognize a familiar footstep at quite a distance. So, as you make your way up the street, your cat should be expecting you. They'll greet you by immediately launching into a litany of grievances and needs—the story of their day. And boy, can they talk a blue streak. After you have been reprimanded for leaving them alone for so long, they inform you (very loudly) that their dish is empty. Interestingly, they never admit to feeling hungry. They are not pleading for food, or even asking nicely for it. Their expectation is that the food should be there. What they want is the option, the choice to eat when they choose, on their timetable, not ours—and to eat the food they prefer. They are simply pointing out the error of your ways. And therein lies the secret of our relationships with cats, as Mark Twain so insightfully suggests—they are slaves to no one.

After the daily scolding and ritualistic re-establishing of the rules of the game, they then offer you demonstrations of affection—loud purring, loving head butts, and even rolling on their back to expose their vulnerable little belly to you. This is now all the more gratifying, and an endearing manifestation of the loyalty and sophistication of the feline mind.

Throughout the pages that follow, I will share the history, folklore, biology, and everything in between that is the world of cats. However, dear reader, I can't promise that I won't dote on my own beloved Kitty, a female chocolate-point Siamese who stole my heart many years ago.

I hope you enjoy.

Kitty

Kitty

Chapter 1

Hiss-tory

THE earliest ancestors of the modern cat appeared twelve million years ago, and cats of all kinds flourished in prehistory. The first domesticated cats probably joined human society about 3000 BC, in Ancient Egypt.

Art on Egyptian temple walls indicates the very high esteem in which cats were held. They were apparently considered very close to the gods. Women adored the cat and copied her luminous eyes in their elaborate makeup with winged kohl eyeliner. When a pet cat died, her owners would shave off their eyebrows to show how deeply she was mourned.

Carved images of cats were believed to have spiritual or even magic powers of protecting human beings, and living cats were often kept by priests or other religious attendants. Their slightest meow or tail twitch was carefully attended to as a portent or omen.

Like a graceful vase, a cat, even
when motionless, seems to flow.
–GEORGE F. WILL

The goddess Isis was always accompanied by a sacred cat, and cats themselves became objects of veneration.

The Egyptian cat goddess, Bast, or Bastet, had the body of a woman and the head of a cat. She was the giver of love and fertility. Temples were consecrated to the worship of cats, and magnificent tombs were built for them. They were believed to possess the powers of the night, because of their ability to see in the dark and the flashing light that was reflected from their eyes. The rising and setting of the moon was also said to be controlled by cats, and they were considered to be the protectors of the dead.

Since the Egyptians considered cats to be powerful and sacred, they were also very valuable. It was forbidden to take them out of the country. Despite this, they were moved illegally, and bought and sold as precious objects.

The Romans kept pet cats, as did the Greeks, and cats appear as images on Greek coins and in Roman mosaics. From the archaeological record, it appears that the Romans brought cats with them when they settled in Britain.

"Thousands of years ago, cats were worshipped as gods. Cats have never forgotten this."
—ANONYMOUS

Cats were also carried to Ireland, perhaps during the Dark Ages. There are pictures of cats and kittens in the famous illuminated manuscript from the eighth century, The Book of Kells.

Norse mythology also had a place for the cat. The love goddess Freya was pulled in her chariot by two black cats, who later became witches, though they still appeared in the form of cats. Worldly wealth was represented symbolically by the image of the cat.

There are no cats in the Old Testament, but the Babylonian Talmud mentions them approvingly as useful for keeping down the mice.

An Islamic tale from the Hadith, a collection of the sayings of the Prophet Mohammed, tells of a cat that was neglected and starved to death by a woman who should have looked after it. In a vision, Mohammed saw her being attacked by the cat—in hell. "You neither fed nor watered this cat. You locked it up," God told her. "Nor did you set it free to eat the insects of the earth."

The moral of the story is that kindness to cats is a duty, because they are good to us.

My favourite story is about Mohammed's beloved cat, Muezza. Mohammed was called to prayer, but noticed the cat was sound asleep, lying on his sleeve. Rather than disturb the cat, he cut off his sleeve. When he returned, the cat is said to have bowed to him in thanks, and so Mohammed guaranteed his pet a place in heaven.

The lore of cats' helpfulness to mankind includes the story of a man, named Sir Henry Wyatt, imprisoned in the Tower of London. Since the jailers often neglected to feed the prisoners, Wyatt might have died of starvation if it had not been for his cat, who killed birds and dropped them into his master's cell, thus saving his life. Wyatt was eventually released, and I think it was because the king was so impressed by the cat's creativity!

There's no need for a piece of sculpture
in a home that has a cat.
—WESLEY BATES

Cats were so important for the control of rodents that by 948 AD, in Wales, they were valued at one penny when they were blind kittens, two pennies while they were growing, and after they had proved their worth by killing a mouse, they doubled in value to four pennies.

Their failure to be mentioned in the Bible brought cats to grief in the Middle Ages. Since they were not in the Good Book, they must be creatures of the Devil, or so the reasoning went. They began to be associated with black magic, and women who had pet cats were often accused of witchcraft. During one particularly intolerant time, many women and their cats were burned at the stake.

But when the bubonic plague swept through Europe, cats were again valued, because they killed the rats that carried the disease. By the time the Renaissance rolled around, almost everyone—including royalty—had cats, and their status grew.

By the time Charles I came to the throne in the seventeenth century, cats were thought to bring good fortune. The king carried a cat everywhere with him, and when it died, he was heard to declare that his luck had gone. The next day he was arrested, and subsequently beheaded by an English soldier named Oliver Cromwell.

Royal favour continued in the reign of Queen Victoria, who owned two Persian cats.

"Civilization is defined by the presence of cats."
–ANONYMOUS

I'll end this chapter with a wonderful little Russian tale about a heroic cat. In the beginning of the twentieth century, before the Russian Revolution, one of the last elders of an Orthodox monastery—a cat lover named Nektary—often told this story:

At the time of the Great Flood, Noah rescued as many people and animals as he could by building his Ark to save them from a watery death. The Ark would thwart the Devil's plan, which was to kill all living things.

He was so angry that he turned himself into a mouse, sneaked aboard the Ark and began to gnaw a hole in the ship's hull. Fortunately a vigilant cat pounced on the mouse and killed it, thus saving mankind and all the animals from destruction.

A cat named Cleo

Chapter 2

Cat-ology

Tails

THE long, flexible tail of the cat is an elegant indicator of its feelings. A curious cat has a softly raised tail. When the tail curls downward, then up again at the tip, it is a calm, contented feline. A twitching tail is a warning sign, and if it twitches just at the tip, the cat is becoming seriously annoyed. A tail tucked in close to the body, or between the legs, is a sure sign of insecurity. Lowered and puffed out, with fur standing on end, it shows a nervous, frightened cat. But when the tail is held high like a sail, with the tip pointing straight up, the cat is offering a joyful hello, and if the whole length is softly quivering, the cat is telling his human that he loves him and wants to be petted.

A wagging cat tail, of course, is not the same thing as a wagging dog tail. A smoothly switching tail can mean the cat is thinking, perhaps coming to a decision about something (the equivalent of a thoughtful frown on a human face). However, a tail lashing rapidly from side to side indicates a furious and possibly even dangerous cat.

According to Simon and Schuster's Guide to Cats, a cat has "245 bones, of which about 20 are in its tail." The tail plays a vital part in the cat's balance and in the "righting reflex" that allows it to land on its feet after falling from a height. The domestic cat is the only species able to hold its tail vertically while walking.

"Do you see that kitten chasing so prettily her own tail? If you could look with her eyes, you might see her surrounded with hundreds of figures performing complex dramas, with tragic and comic issues, long conversations, many characters, many ups and downs of fate."

–RALPH WALDO EMERSON

Whiskers

CAT'S whiskers, or vibrissae, are sensing devices that provide a wealth of information. If you touch them, the cat will instinctively draw back and close her eyes.

A happy cat that wants to be cuddled will be holding her whiskers in a curved, forward position. If she is irritated, her whiskers will point backwards.

"I believe cats to be spirits come to earth. A cat, I am sure, could walk on a cloud without coming through."
–JULES VERNE

Much like human fingerprints, no two feline nose pads are alike. On either side, a cat has four rows of "beard" whiskers. The upper rows can move independently of the bottom two, and they are highly sophisticated sensors, reacting to the lightest touch or changes in air currents and the environment.

Even in the dark, a cat can make its way by using its whiskers to determine if a space is big enough to pass through.

An adult cat also has whiskers on the backs of its forelegs. You may expect company, it is said, if a cat fixes its whiskers.

Eyes

IN relation to their body size, cats have the largest eyes of any mammal, but they don't have any eyelashes, only eyebrow whiskers. Cats can see as far as 120 feet away. Their peripheral vision can take in about 285 degrees—but they don't observe detail particularly well. They are also thought to see a limited range of colours.

Cats need only a sixth of the light that humans require to see clearly, so they have excellent night vision. Their extensive peripheral vision and binocular vision enable them to judge distances accurately. They respond to the sight of something moving, instantly finding it with their eyes, and this helps them to catch it, if it is a mouse.

"Who can believe that there is no soul behind those luminous eyes!"

-THÉOPHILE GAUTIER

Still, a cat cannot see directly under its nose, which is why they cannot seem to find tidbits on the floor.

Isn't it interesting that we even call one of our precious stones a cat's-eye?

"It always gives me a shiver when I see a cat seeing what I can't see."

-A CAT LOVER

Ears

CATS have thirty-two muscles in each ear, and each ear pivots, independently, 180 degrees. The cat can turn its ears quickly to focus on different sounds, and its hearing is extremely acute and sensitive. A cat can hear sounds that are up to two octaves higher than those audible to humans, even in the ultrasonic range, but its ears are less sensitive to lower frequencies—which may explain why some domestic cats are more responsive to female voices than to male voices.

"When Kitty washes behind her ears,
we'll soon be tasting heaven's tears."
–OLD RHYME

Newborn kittens have firmly closed eyes for the first few days of their life, and they also have closed ear canals for nine days.

A cat can express many shades of emotion with her flexible ears. If they are flattened to her head, she is very angry. If they are pointing forward, she is curious or very interested.

"It is a bold mouse that makes
her nest in the cat's ear."

-DANISH PROVERB

The Feline Form

CATS walk on their toes, not the soles of their feet—no other animal does that. And like only two other animals (the giraffe and the camel), a cat moves its left foreleg together with its left hind leg, then both right legs together, when it runs or walks.

*"If a fish is the movement of water embodied,
then a cat is a diagram and pattern
of subtle air."*

-DORIS LESSING

Cats are also extraordinary jumpers. A startled cat can jump up to five times its height straight up into the air. If you could do that, you would be jumping thirty feet up from a standing start!

Have you ever wondered why a cat (or a dog) turns around and around in circles before lying down to sleep? They are making their beds—the action is an instinctive one dating back to the time when they slept in tall grass and had to flatten it into a comfortable nest.

A cat rolling over to show her belly is offering a display of affection. See, she is saying. I totally trust you. And a cat that sleeps on its back with all four paws in the air knows with certainty that his home is safe and secure.

"How we behave here towards cats below determines our status in heaven."

-ROBERT HEINLEIN

Kitty

Chapter 3

The Cat's Meow

Y ES, I talked to my cat! Most people do. And most people also believe that their pets both understand and talk back. The French novelist Colette, whose remarks about cats have been noted elsewhere in these pages, was a lover of cats. Once she stopped to greet a cat in the street, and the cat answered with a polite meow. The writer and the cat then carried on a conversation, talking and meowing back and forth. After a few minutes of this, Colette turned to her companion and exclaimed, "Enfin! Quelqu'un qui parle français!" (At last! Someone who speaks French!).

Animal behaviourists agree that cats do communicate with people, but that doesn't mean they communicate like people.

Cats have about a hundred different vocalizations and sounds. And by the way, a cat almost never meows at another cat—meowing is the sound they use for communicating with humans.

Cats also react to the tone of your voice. They can tell if you're happy, upset, or angry with them. And that meow is usually trying to tell you something. If you respond to a cat's vocalizations—answering them with meows if you like, though words are more natural for most humans (Colette excluded)—you establish a rapport and begin to build a language both of you understand, which you will use to create a relationship over the years.

Purring is perhaps a more sophisticated form of communication. Cats purr when they are happy and content, but they do sometimes purr when they are in pain. A mother cat purrs loudly when her kittens are being born (though she does yelp with pain at the moment of the actual birth) and the kittens respond with their own purring after a week or so—a communication that may be the equivalent of "More milk, please."

And as noted earlier, researchers believe that the act of purring may help develop or even heal bone. If purring does help build strong bones, it may be that it has the same positive effect as ultrasound treatments on humans.

It is also said that cats purr at twenty-six cycles per second—the same frequency as an idling diesel engine. I can only tell you that when my cat Kitty curled up next to my ear at night, I believed this to be a fact.

Mark Twain was a writer who loved to pull your leg. He once wrote about Jim Baker, a miner in California who claimed he could translate animal languages into good English. Some cats, Baker reported, were eloquent speakers, with large vocabularies and a high level of education. Others liked to talk a lot, but really had nothing to say—they were just showing off. Still, though they could speak in a refined way, occasionally they forgot the nicer points of grammar:

You say a cat uses good grammar. Well, a cat does—but you let a cat get excited once, you let a cat get to pulling fur with another cat on a shed, and you'll hear grammar that will give you lockjaw. Ignorant people think it's the noise which fighting cats make that is so aggravating, but it ain't so; it's the sickening grammar they use.

A meow massages the heart.

–STEWART MCMILLAN

They say that a sure indication of a mediocre mind is the belief that everything can be explained. Well, not everything can. But I, like many pet lovers, believe that a special bond develops between humans and our animal companions—a bond that allows us to communicate quite well across the species.

Greater minds than mine share that view. For example, Jane Goodall, the activist primatologist, had no formal academic training when at age twenty-six, she went into the jungles of Africa. What she did have was a lifelong passion for animals. From a very early age, Jane would wait for hours in the henhouse—to see where an egg came from. She read about animals, and by the age of ten, she was determined to go to Africa and find Tarzan. Instead, she met the renowned Dr. Richard Leakey, who quizzed her about primates—and because she had done so much reading, she answered him well and he gave her a job as his assistant, despite her lack of formal academic credentials. Jane Goodall still talks with passion about the chimps that she came to know and love:

Their communication—kissing, holding hands, slapping each other on the back, tickling, laughing—is just like ours. And they know grief and sorrow and fear—mental as well as physical suffering... It's about intuition. Of course, when I first went out, I couldn't talk about their personality or minds or reasoning power—at that time it was a scientific "fact" that only human beings had these things. Only humans used and made tools, and certainly, only humans had emotions. If you ignored these things, you were guilty of anthropomorphism. But I hadn't been to university, so I didn't know those things.

In her naïveté, Goodall discovered what the scientists had refused to see. Perhaps that same "naïveté" is why pet owners are able to communicate with their animal companions—because we don't know any better.

I also explored some of these ideas with one of the world's leading primatologists, Frans de Waal, at Emory University, where a recent study has shown that primates in the wild cooperate to achieve goals and then share the rewards. The researchers called it "calculated reciprocity" and said it was comparable to the human system of payment for labour and labour for payment. One of de Waal's books, Good Natured: The Origins of Right and Wrong in Humans and Other Animals, poses the most fundamental questions about us: Is morality human? Are humans humane, and is that what sets us apart from our primate ancestors?

The scientists have no absolute answers, of course, but that doesn't mean they can't disagree. Richard Dawkins argues that we are born selfish and must learn generosity and altruism. The late Stephen Jay Gould wondered whether animals cannot be as loving as any human: "Why should our nastiness be the baggage of an ape-ish past and our kindness uniquely human?"

> *If animals could speak, the dog would*
> *be a blundering outspoken fellow, but the*
> *cat would have the rare grace of never*
> *saying a word too much.*
>
> –MARK TWAIN

Now, this is not to say that animals do not share other, less desirable, traits as well. They can be selfish and mean and aggressive, and they will kill to survive. And when it comes to humans making moral judgement calls, we assume that some kind of intellectual motivation and intention underlie the behaviour. But is that necessarily so? What about primates or other animals? Is there such a thing as friendship between animals? Or intimacy? Or are we really just anthropomorphizing and projecting our human interpretations to explain what we don't understand? Wherever you stand on the questions, it's hard to deny that animals often display caring, which the scientists call "reciprocal altruism"—caring for others and risking or sacrificing to do it.

De Waal's argument that moral behaviour may indeed exist in animals poses a profound challenge to Darwin's theory that traits evolve because the bearer is better off with them than without them. So how would moral behaviour such as self-sacrifice evolve? What's in it for us to be humane or for animals to be moral? It's not clear that these traits have anything to do with ensuring survival for us or for them.

You see, de Wall and other scientists believe that morality is grounded in biology. Therefore, animals can be moral too. But to communicate intentions and feelings is one thing; to explain what is right and wrong is another. De Waal concedes that animals are not moral philosophers, at least by our standards. Then again, our track record isn't great either.

A chimpanzee sharing food with a disabled member of the tribe is not much different from our own willingness to serve meals at the local soup kitchen. Altruism starts with an obligation to oneself. When that moral obligation widens to family, tribe, or nation, then we have moral beings—animal or human—don't we?

Michael Hackenberger, who owned a zoo and rescue centre in Bowmanville, Ontario, was an adviser to the author of a book that became one of my all-time favourites—The Final Confession of Mabel Stark. It's a lovely "faux biography" of a woman renowned as the greatest female tiger trainer in history. I immediately loved Mabel because of her obsession with large cats.

Mabel was real, but the details of her life and times were so sketchy that the author, Robert Hough, used literary licence to colour in between the lines. We learn that Mabel was an orphan, a nurse, a wife—and, on repeated occasions, a mental patient. She was also an "exotic" dancer along with her primary talent as a world-famous lion and tiger tamer. But her legendary success in the ring is attributed to her humane treatment of the animals, which was effective although much less flashy than the approach her male counterparts took. And that is of course the lesson—her belief that the animals, like humans, have emotions and feelings and moods, and that, though the words may be absent, we do communicate with the animals once a bond of trust and respect has been established. You can only hope that her real life was as layered—and as full of love (most of it for her big kitties)—as this fictionalized account presents.

I have studied many philosophers and many cats. The wisdom of cats is infinitely superior.

–HIPPOLYTE TAINE

The intimacy of our separateness is at the core of Mabel's story. While the emotional bond with her cats was deep, there is also the obvious fact that she was human and they were not. Still, there's an undeniable love and affection that easily clears the barriers of biology.

Michael Hackenberger also introduced me to a remarkable big cat. Some of you will have heard the name Bongo. This graceful and gentle lion was a bona fide movie star, stealing scenes from his human in movies such as George of the Jungle (1997).

Bongo and I had something in common. In the summer of 2001, we were both battling cancer, and I went to spend a day at the Bowmanville Zoo to say goodbye to my friend. Bongo had been a guest on my TV show many times, accompanied, of course, by Michael, his friend and teacher.

I talked with Michael then about this special relationship between man and cat:

PW: What was so incredibly special about Bongo?

MH: He was one in a million. I wish 1 could say I'll train another one like him. I'm not going to. He's exceptional. He's like a Wayne Gretzky. He's like a Michael Jordan. He's like an Albert Einstein. He's a one-off. He really is.

PW: Is he smart? Is he intelligent?

MH: He is "intelligent" in how we measure "intelligence"—

by a whole bunch of measurements. He's able to generalize across a wide variety of different environments. He's able to actually figure out things. So on set...OK...we need him to jump through the window, run up the stairs, and then jump on and pretend to kill someone. So that's three separate things...

PW: And he could do all that, in order...

MH: Yes.

PW: He was an amazing movie star in that sense because he didn't really put people in danger...although you always offer that proviso, "A wild animal is a wild animal."

MH: They are what they are. But he never, ever betrayed that trust. Never.

PW. So what is it? It's just a character?

MH: Character...personality...I think "character" is a good word. What makes great people great? Character.

Pamela visited the zoo in the early Fall of 2001, and her feline friend died soon after.

Bongo the Lion

Watching Michael with Bongo and with other large cats and animals—especially the highly intelligent elephants—is evidence that man and animal can and do communicate. Some of the behaviour is learned. These animals are trained and rewarded for their actions, eventually beginning to perform on command. But even when he is not in the ring or on the set, Michael can give complicated instructions or messages to his animal charges—and they understand. I have watched, and marvelled, as they carried out his wishes.

There is no doubt in my mind that they were in profound communication with their human friend.

From Timothy Findley's memoir, Inside Memory

I had another flash of insight about Tiresias which came because Mottyl lay at my leg last night while I was reading in bed—and I could sense her instinctive knowledge of me as a creature—as being another creature—that aspect of "animal" and "man" that is always missed. To them, we are not always overlords and "god" whose whims and gifts they depend on. I listened to her speaking to me in that semi-magical way that cats communicate (purring), and I thought: she accepts me as more than her feeder—her eyes—her opener of doors. I am more than her warmth and security—I am her companion in a far deeper sense—on an entirely other plane than the one I so glibly imagine or accept.

I am her fellow animal. We have a relationship that is as complex from her point of view as any I could ever have with another human being-and this thought made me see that our relationship is also, therefore, complex to me.

A sleepy cat

Chapter 4
Kitty Lore

Everyone has heard about the nine lives of the cat. This folk saying goes back to a time when the religious symbolism of the number three was very powerful, and as the "trinity of trinities", the number nine was considered lucky. It follows that cats were also considered lucky because they are so adept at avoiding danger.

Cats are small, light, and lithe. They can quickly climb trees, fall from great heights without hurting themselves, and run away from enemies. To superstitious people, it might easily seem that their chances were better—nine times better—than other creatures.

A cat has nine lives. For three he plays, for three he strays, and for the last three, he stays.
—ENGLISH PROVERB

When a cat falls from a high place, he is said to be able to land on his feet. In fact, the cat can open his legs out into a parachute shape, which slows his fall and lessens the impact when he does hit the ground. Their fine sense of balance does the rest. Even when they don't actually land on their feet, they get back up very fast!

Another "life-saving" feature of cat physiology may be their purring, as we've mentioned before. According to the recent theory, a cat's purr is a natural healing mechanism. (And I can attest, they can heal their humans too!) Whatever the reason, the myth about their nine lives has become part of our lives and our everyday language.

It has long been believed that the cat has a great influence on the weather. The dog, an attendant of the storm king Odin, was a symbol of wind, while cats came to symbolize down-pouring rain. They say that witches who rode on storms took the form of cats, and there are hundreds of other examples. If a cat continually looks out a window, rain is on the way. A sneezing cat means rain on the way, and three sneezes in a row portend a cold for the cat's owner. A cat running wildly about, darting here and dashing around in excitement, means wind or a storm on the way. When she settles down, the storm will soon blow itself out. A cat sleeping with all four paws tucked under means cold weather ahead, according to English superstition. And if she sits with her back to the fire, frost is coming. Almost all of a cat's behaviours, in fact, are weather predictors— even washing behind its ears!

The cat has too much spirit to have no heart.
–ERNEST MENAUL

Sailors, who risked their lives on the ocean, believed in many spells and superstitions that they hoped would keep them safe. It was very important to have a cat on board their ship, particularly a cat with six or seven toes on each paw. But cats in general were bearers of good luck. A cat running across a sailor's path as he boarded the ship was a good omen, and if his wife kept a black cat as a pet, it was said to ensure that her husband would return safely from the sea. Black cats were therefore precious, and sometimes even stolen from their rightful owners!

Yet, the word "cat" itself was unlucky, and sailors would not allow the little syllable to pass their lips. And if the ship's cat was black, it must have no white hairs.

Cats were thought to be able to either prevent disaster, or bring it down around people's ears in a moment. If a cat was thrown overboard, a violent storm would blow up at once. As late as the nineteenth century, a ship's cargo could not be insured against loss if there was no cat on board.

But what about bad luck? Some people think white cats bring bad luck, especially if you chance to see one at night. The power of a cat to heal the sick was greatly respected in Renaissance Italy—so much so that if the cat wanted to go out when a person lay sick in the house, it meant the patient would die.

Cat sneezes are said to predict the rain, and also bring good luck. But it is bad luck to carry a cat across a stream.

In Britain and Australia, black cats are lucky, while in many parts of Europe and in the United States, they are unlucky. Tortoiseshell cats will bring British cat owners luck. Blue cats do the same in Russia. Irish lore probably carried the unlucky black cat to the United States—in Ireland, if a black cat crosses your path by moonlight, you will die.

An American folk belief maintains that you should put your cat in through the window when you move to a new home—to make sure it will never leave. And when a young Pennsylvania Dutch couple goes home from their wedding, they may find a cat in the cradle as a spell to bring them children.

The fog comes / on little cat feet. /
It sits looking over harbor and city /
on silent haunches / and then, moves on.
–CARL SANDBURG

The cat has been the companion of the human race since the long-forgotten beginnings of our time on earth, and it is no wonder that her powerful spirit has created many myths and legends about her mystery and secret knowledge.

Take Aesop's story of "belling the cat." The mice held a general assembly to discuss how they might defend themselves against the cat. After several suggestions were debated, a mouse of experience and standing got up and said: "I think I have hit upon a plan which will ensure our future safety. We will fasten a bell around the neck of our enemy, the cat, which by its tinkling will alert us when she is near." Everyone thought it was a wonderful idea. A bell to warn them of the cat's approach! All agreed that the problem was solved. But then another mouse got to his feet. He had seen a flaw in the plan. Who would bell the cat?

There is a particular mythology surrounding the Siamese. With their sooty faces, tails, and legs, they were once called "the shadow of the ancient gods' hands." According to the legend, a god picked up a pale cat and stroked it, and the blessing of the deity's fingertips left a mark on a cat, which was ever after considered sacred. My Siamese cat's markings are truly beautiful, whether they are the traces of divine hands or not!

Excerpt from The Cat's Pajamas, by Lenore Fleischer

When God made the world, He chose to put animals in it, and decided to give each whatever it wanted. All the animals formed a long line before His throne, and the cat quietly went to the end of the line. To the elephant and the bear He gave strength; to the rabbit and the deer, swiftness; to the owl, the ability to see at night; to the birds and the butterflies, great beauty; to the fox, cunning; to the monkey, intelligence; to the dog, loyalty;

to the lion, courage; to the otter, playfulness. And all these were things the animals begged of God. At last he came to the end of the line, and there sat the little cat, waiting patiently. "What will YOU have?" God asked the cat.

The cat shrugged modestly. "Oh, whatever scraps you have left over. I don't mind."

"But I'm God. I have everything left over."

"Then I'll have a little of everything, please."

And God gave a great shout of laughter at the cleverness of this small animal, and gave the cat everything she asked for, adding grace and elegance and, only for her, a gentle purr that would always attract humans and assure her a warm and comfortable home.

But he took away her false modesty.

Kitty

Silva and Kitty

Chapter 5
Kitty Lit

CATS have served as both comfort and inspiration for writers throughout time; Stephen King, W.B. Yeats, T.S. Eliot, and Lewis Carroll all loved and admired cats. Ernest Hemingway once offered an explanation of the special connection between writers and cats: "A cat has absolute emotional honesty: human beings, for one reason or another, may hide their feelings, but a cat does not."

A cat in the writing room is a quieting influence, or a distraction if the writer wants an excuse not to write. As Dan Greenburg once said, "Cats are dangerous companions for writers because cat-watching is a near-perfect method of writing-avoidance."

Authors like cats because they are such quiet, lovable, wise creatures and cats like authors for the same reasons.

–ROBERTSON DAVIES

Of course, they do jump on the desk, lie across your papers, and meow to be let out or in. Yet, as Barbara Holland writes, "A catless writer is almost inconceivable. It's a perverse taste, really, since it would be easier to write with a herd of buffalo in the room than even one cat; they make nests in the notes and bite the end of the pen and walk on the typewriter keys."

The late author Timothy Findley was a cat lover. From his memoir, Inside Memory, one gets a glimpse of the very close bond that existed between writer and cat in this instance. Findley confesses to hours spent crawling around on his hands and knees—bum in the air—to garner a "cat's eye view of the world." As a writer, he said it gave him a fresh perspective. His observations of his own cat allowed him to create the cat Mottyl, an unforgettable wise character in his novel Not Wanted on the Voyage. In Inside Memory, he wrote:

I look down, now, from this writing, and see her
at the centre of the rug and she is brooding—and,
because I have turned my chair to see her—she hears
this; one ear lifts back in my direction. This is subtle—
but absolute. What I do next will govern what she
does next. If I leave the room, her hearing will follow
me. No matter where I go in the house, she will "follow"
me that way. I am an extension of her nerve ends.

She has a wisdom of her own that has nothing to do
with thought as we know it. Nor with "instinct" as we
describe it for ourselves. Whatever it is, it lies on that same
plane where we are creatures together in this one place
where we share our existence. As human beings, we have
forgotten how to play our role in that dimension. Why?

How can it be that Mottyl is so utterly herself—when with all my human intellect—I so often fail to be myself at all?

If the world can be divided into dog people and cat people, it's clear that the vast majority of writers are cat people. Take Duncan Campbell Scott, for example. Born in Ottawa in 1862, he is widely considered as one of Canada's great Confederation poets. Scott was prolific, crafting such works as "At the Cedars," "Enigma" and "Night Hymns on Lake Nipigon"—and he wasn't ashamed to say that he was "addicted to cats." A cat named Skookum was always draped across his knees as he wrote, and he expressed approval of Mark Twain's habit of renting a few cats to prowl the hotel room wherever he was on tour.

In fact, there is a documented story of Twain renting three kittens from a local farm woman just to amuse him and keep him company one summer. He spent the afternoons on the porch watching them chase grasshoppers and butterflies, and their curiosity and playfulness were a constant source of joy for him. "Next to a wife whom I idolize," Twain wrote to his wife, Olivia, "give me a cat—an old cat with kittens."

Hal Holbrook, an actor who has performed as Mark Twain all over the world, described Samuel Clemens (Twain's real name) as a "soul seeking the truth...which can be a lonely journey." Perhaps Mark Twain recognized something of his own skeptical, ironic view when he looked into the eyes of a cat. At any rate, he called himself a "cat expert" and during his lifetime had cats named Buffalo Bill, Satan (and her kitten Sin), Abner, Fraulein, Blatherskite, Beelzebub, Tammany, Apollinaris, Sour Mash, and Zoroaster. Twain chose these unusual names, he said, to "practice the children in large and difficult styles of pronunciation."

From "Blackie in Antarctica"—Margaret Atwood

Oh Blackie, named bluntly
and without artifice by small girls,
leaping from roof to roof
in doll's bonnet and pinafore,
Oh sly fur-faced idol,
who endured worship and mauling,
often without scratching,
Oh yowling moon

addict, devious foundling,
neurotic astrologer
who predicted disaster
by then creating it,

Oh midnight-coloured
faithful companion of midnight,
Oh follow hog,
with your breath of raw liver,
where are you now?

—*Margaret Atwood*

Jules Verne was probably the most popular novelist of his time in the world, although he'd been a poet first. For forty years, he had an agreement with his publisher to produce two novels a year for life. When he died in 1905, he was some twelve or fifteen books ahead of schedule, having completed more than one hundred works—all unique and all scrupulously researched. Verne was proud of his prescience—a truly accurate word in his case in that his ideas often preceded science. And like so many great minds, he loved and respected the cat. In his words, "I believe cats to be spirits come to earth. A cat, I am sure, could walk on a cloud without coming through."

Well-known and well-loved cats include the ones depicted in Old Possum's Book of Practical Cats, by poet T.S. Eliot, and Puss in Boots, from the classic fairy tale by the French writer Charles Perrault. Edward Lear, a Victorian author and humorist, wrote several silly—yet memorable—songs about cats. Lear's greatest friend in life was his cat Foss, who lived with the writer for seventeen years and inspired many of his works. You'll remember the ending of his most famous story. An owl and a pussy-cat sail off to purchase a ring from a pig with a ring at the end of his nose. The unlikely couple are married and live happily ever after, dancing by the light of the moon.

From "The Owl and the Pussy-Cat"—Edward Lear

The Owl and the Pussy-cat went to sea
In a beautiful pea-green boat:
They took some honey and plenty of money,
Wrapped up in a five-pound note.
The Owl looked up to the stars above,

And sang to a small guitar,
'Oh lovely pussy, O pussy my love,
What a beautiful pussy you are,
You are,
You are!'

—*Edward Lear*

In The Cat That Walked by Himself, the origins of the ancient bargain struck between cat and human are related by the great Rudyard Kipling. The independent, solitary feline would not agree to live with people on the slavish terms that the dog had accepted; he would take a place in the society of primitive men that allowed him the freedom to be himself. Kipling's own illustration for the tale shows the black shape of a cat walking away, the tips of his ears pointing downward in grumpy displeasure, tail held high but waving as he lashes it from side to side to show how little he cares.

Classic cats from children's books include Dr. Seuss's The Cat in the Hat and, of course, the disappearing Cheshire cat from Lewis Carroll's Alice's Adventures in Wonderland.

Alice was published in 1865. Over the subsequent 137 years, it has delighted generations of children and adults. The pleasure I remember from reading it as a child has not diminished with time, I am pleased to report. I recently picked up a beautiful red leather-bound copy and was happy to rediscover the Cheshire cat, which you'll recall, frequently vanishes from sight, leaving behind only its grin.

From "Alice's Adventures in Wonderland"

"Please would you tell me," said Alice, a little timidly, for she was not quite sure whether it was good manners for her to speak first, "why your cat grins like that?"

"It's a Cheshire cat," said the Duchess, "and that's why."

"I didn't know that Cheshire cats always grinned, in fact I didn't know that cats could grin."

"They all can," said the Duchess; "and most of 'em do."

"I don't know of any that do," Alice said very politely, feeling quite pleased to have got into a conversation.

"You don't know much," said the Duchess; "and that's a fact."

The Cat only grinned when it saw Alice. It looked good-natured, she thought: still it had very long claws and a great many teeth, so she felt that it ought to be treated with respect.

"Cheshire Puss," she began, rather timidly, as she did not at all know whether it would like the name: however, it only grinned a little wider"... I wish you wouldn't keep appearing and vanishing so suddenly: you make one quite giddy."

"All right," said the Cat, and this time it vanished quite slowly, beginning with the end of the tail, and ending with the grin, which remained some time after the rest of it had gone.

"Well! I've often seen a cat without a grin," thought Alice, "but a grin without a cat! It's the most curious thing I ever saw in my life!"

—Lewis Carroll

Chapter 6

The Comfort of Cats

HUMANS show affection in so many different ways. We may greet our friends and loved ones with a hug, then instinctively rub their backs or pat their arms as we stand looking into their eyes, declaring how much we have missed them, how glad we are to see them again, or how wonderful they look.

One of the oldest human needs is having someone to wonder where you are when you don't come home at night.

–MARGARET MEAD

Everyone needs to feel needed. Everyone needs to have something or someone to care for. Kids caress their dolls and teddy bears, and a parent instinctively strokes a child's feverish forehead. Watch a child petting a dog or gently stroking a cat, or observe an elderly person enjoying the companionship of a furry friend, and you'll see what a delight it is, for both animal and human. It seems that for the human spirit, nurture is a biological imperative. And often the simplest of pleasures answers this basic human need.

Touch is no less important for people who are alone and the elderly. The simple act of stroking a cat brings comfort. As British researcher Dr. David Purdie says, the human skeleton actually needs stimulation or it becomes weak. "Purring," he says, "could be the cat's way of providing that stimulation for its own bones." Purdie even speculates that a cat's purring might be helpful in strengthening elderly human bones!

Medical research makes a convincing case for the power of touch. For many people who live alone, or for the elderly, pets can provide a reason for living. Pets make us more active, provide a routine, give us something to look forward to, and inculcate a sense of responsibility. Tests have even revealed that stroking dogs and cats can lower our blood pressure and heart rate.

Caring for a pet teaches a child about responsibility. They learn that animals not only offer love and loyalty but feel pain and hunger, and face illness, even death—knowledge that teaches a child the realities of life. As a child, I witnessed several animal births and observed the instinctive nature of a mother's love. It was an unforgettable lesson. But these days there is also scientific evidence that children with pets develop better social skills and hold a greater respect for all living things.

You can't look at a sleeping cat and be tense.
–JANE PAULEY

Pets play many roles in our lives—a family member, a friend, a babysitter for children, a companion, a toy, a playmate, a worker to be commanded, and even a fashion accessory. But most people have a pet for companionship. They want some creature to whom they can give affection—and from whom they will receive affection in return.

In a cat's eyes, all things belong to cats.

–ENGLISH PROVERB

In fact, as of 2023, 66% of U.S. households own a pet. That's over 86.9 million homes! Of these pet owners, 44.5% of households own dogs, and 29% of households own cats. According to VetSource, 80% of pet owners claim their pet can sense their mood; 50% of pet owners talk to their pets; 45% of pet owners allow their pet to sleep in their bed;

and 65% of pet owners take more photos of their dogs than their friends and family! If these statistics don't tell us already, it is evident that the pet gives us a sense of comfort.

As a child, I read The Diary of a Young Girl, by Anne Frank. I could not imagine—no child in my small town in the fifties and sixties could have imagined—what it must have been like for her: the forced confinement, the sadness of being alone together, hiding in fear from the terror of discovery. Some of the older folks in my town had fled such brutal and repressive regimes, but they seldom spoke of it. These topics were certainly not part of any social studies class I ever attended.

Unaware of the place in history that would be hers, Anne wondered in the pages of her diary whether anyone would ever care about the musings of a young girl. She shrugged off the question, declaring wisely that paper has more patience than people, and that the diary would be her friend until she found a real one:

The Diary Of A Young Girl by Anne Frank

To enhance the image of this long-awaited friend in my imagination, I don't want to jot down facts in this diary the way most people would do. But I want the diary to be my friend, and I'm going to call this friend Kitty. I hope I will be able to confide everything to you, as I have never been able to confide in anyone, and I hope you will be a great source of comfort and support. I can hardly wait for those moments when I am able to write in you. I am so glad I brought you along.

Between June 12, 1942 (Anne's thirteenth birthday), and August 1, 1944, she wrote to her "friend Kitty" about the suffering and humiliations of a life of persecution. Anne and her family lived in hiding, crowded together without privacy, and in those hard days she often recalled the

Moortje, my cat, was the only living creature I said goodbye to... I miss her every minute of the day, and no one knows how often I think of her; whenever I do, my eyes fill with tears... I can also understand my homesickness and yearning for Moortje. The whole time I've been here, I've longed unconsciously—and at times consciously—for trust, love, and physical affection. This longing may change in intensity, but it's always there.

—Anne Frank, The Diary of a Young Girl

comfort offered by her dear pet cat, which had to be left behind when they took refuge in the secret annex.

Three days after Anne's last entry in the diary, the eight people held captive in the secret annex were arrested. They were taken to a prison in Amsterdam, then deported to the concentration camps. Anne was taken to Auschwitz and then on to Bergen-Belsen, where she died of typhus about a month before the camps were liberated.

Anne Frank's diary was found by two women working in the building where the family had hidden. After the war, when it became clear Anne was dead, it was handed over—unread—to her father, Otto, who had survived his imprisonment. He decided to share his daughter's diary with the world.

Florence Nightingale was another young woman whose life story fascinated me when I was a young girl with plenty of time to read. When she returned to England from the Crimea, where she had served as a nurse in charge of a military hospital, Nightingale's own health was poor. Although she was often confined to bed, she "found solace in the society of pussy-cats." These constant companions "lay on her pillow, curled themselves round her neck, upset her ink, and left paw marks on her papers."

When her cats had kittens, she gave them away as a special favour to carefully chosen homes. On the following pages is a transcript of a letter written by Miss Nightingale, offering a character reference for one of her cats.

Florence Nightingale's Cat

30 South St. 13 Dec. 1875

Dear Mrs. Frost,

Mrs. Wilson is so good as to invite me to write to you about my Angora Tom-cat (who answers to the name of Mr. White)— now hers.

Mr. White has never made a dirt in his life: but he has been brought up to go to a pan, with sand in it. You must have patience with him, till he has been taught to go out-of-doors for his wants.

He has always been shut up at night: (in a large pantry) to prevent his being lost. And I believe he ought to always be shut up at night: for this reason. (I think you must keep him in the house for two or three days till he knows his kind mistress: & the place: for fear he should run away & try to get back to me.) And perhaps if you could give him a pan with sand in it for the first night or two, it might be better.

He has always been used to having his meals by himself like a gentleman on a plate put upon a 'tablecloth' (on old newspaper) spread on the floor. He is not greedy: has never stolen anything: and never drags his bones off his newspapers. But I am sorry to say he always lived well: he has bones, & milk, in the morning: after 7 o'clock dinner he has remains of fish not fish bones or chicken— or game-bones: which he eats like a gentleman off the plate in my room, as I have described:

& never asks for more— than a little broken meat, &
milk, when he is shut up at night: & a large jar of fresh
water (which he can't upset) always on the floor for him.

He is the most affectionate and intelligent cat
I have ever had: is much fonder of the society of
Christians than of cats: likes of all things to be done
in a room with me: (but makes acquaintances with the
little dog of a baby friend of ours): & when his own
litter sister cat died, he refused food & almost broke his
heart. He washes and dresses two little kits we have here
(of his) himself. I never saw a Tom-cat do this before.

You will see that Mr. White is black now. But when
he is in the country, he is white as the driven snow.
He is 10 months old.

I have written a long letter about him: but in short, I recommend him to your kind care: I am.

Yours faithfully,
Florence Nightingale

—Florence Nightingale

Not surprisingly, when Florence Nightingale died in her home at the age of ninety on August 13, 1910, it was found that she had made provision for her cats in her will.

Love, in any form, is a precious commodity.
Don't let anyone tell you loving a cat is silly.
–A CAT LOVER

I have been told that the ancient Egyptian word for cat was mau, which means "to see," and cats do allow us to see ourselves as no other friend can. For that reason, they are teachers—and much more. An Irish legend would have it, cats' eyes are windows enabling us to see into another world.

They are also windows because their presence allows a gentle light to brighten the dark corners of our lives where troubles can fester. Charles Dickens, the great historian of the troubled heart, had two beloved cats, William and Williamina, and he fully understood their worth. "What greater gift," he wrote, "than the love of a cat?" Our cats, it seems, possess deep reservoirs of peace and strength from which we too can draw comfort each day.

A cat named Romeo

Chapter 7

Famous Feline Names and Namers

"The Naming of Cats is a difficult matter. It isn't just one of your holiday games, You may think at first I'm mad as a hatter, when I tell you, a cat must have THREE DIFFERENT NAMES.

–T.S. ELIOT

ABOVE are the opening lines from "The Naming of Cats." According to Eliot's poem, from Old Possum's Book of Practical Cats (1939), every cat must have three names: one "sensible, everyday" name that his human family gives him ("such as Peter, Augustus, Alonzo, or James"); another "name that is particular" and will never belong to any other cat; and, finally, the name that no human will ever know—or ever guess—and that the cat will never confess.

Just for the record, T.S. Eliot's cat's first two names were George and Pushdragon.

*One for a secret, one for a riddle, name
puss twice and befuddle the Devil.*
–OLD RHYME

An old folk belief held the knowledge that a person's or an animal's real name gave magic power to the knower. And cats, of course, were often thought to be inhabited by witches. So a secret name was given to the cat—a name no outsider would ever learn—and thus the family would be protected against evil entering the house (and the cat would be safe).

The late James Mason, a screen star, was a true cat lover. With his wife, Pamela Kellino, he wrote The Cats in Our Lives, and he illustrated the book with his own drawings of their cats Zeke, Baby, Stink, Angus, Silky, Folly, Lady Leeds, Tree, Archibald, Buchanan, Princess Squaddle, and Flower Face.

Marilyn Monroe called her feline Mitsou. Elizabeth Taylor's cat was named Jeepers Creepers, and Doris Day, predictably, called hers Punky. James Dean had a cat friend named Marcus.

Cats do not have to be shown how to have a good time,
for they are unfailingly ingenious in that respect.
–JAMES MASON

Billy Crystal's cat, Mittens, enjoyed "fishing and computer programming", according to the actor. Steve Martin called his cat Dr. Carlton B. Forbes, while Wilt Chamberlain, the basketball great, had identical black cats called Zip and Zap.

Taylor Swift named her cats after her favourite TV show characters, Meredith Grey and Olivia Benson, and says that it's a daily struggle for her to not buy more cats. Katy

Perry has a cat named after her celebrity persona, Kitty Purry, and she even went on to release a perfume line inspired by her cats. Britney Spears' cat's name is Wendy, and Jennifer Lopez named her feline friend Hendrix.

Politicians have long been cat lovers, it seems. Abraham Lincoln had four of them in the White House. Theodore Roosevelt's Slippers had six toes on each paw, and often appeared at diplomatic dinners—though that was before cats became a regular part of the White House photo op phenomenon. Calvin Coolidge, the thirtieth president of the United States, liked cats and would often walk around his office with his yellow cat draped over his shoulder like a fur piece. Charles de Gaulle called his chat Gris-Gris, and Ronald Reagan called his Cleo. And despite an allergy, Bill Clinton had Socks (and Buddy the dog).

Sir Isaac Newton, it is said, invented the cat flap for his cat Spithead. The Spanish for cat door is gatera, and a small hinged door was often cut into the doors of Spanish houses to allow the resident cats to go in and out at their pleasure. It was also used (so they say) by young lovers who were not allowed to meet. Lying on the floor inside, the young woman would hold conversations with her friend, who would lie on the step outside and peek through the flap. The wise Prophet Mohammed cherished his cat Muezza, and Nostradamus, the French astrologer, had a cat named Grimalkin.

Artists like cats; soldiers like dogs.

–DESMOND MORRIS

Queen Victoria had one named White Heather, and Koko, the famous gorilla that learned to talk through sign language, had a pet kitten called All Ball.

Jay Leno inexplicably chose the name Cheeseler. Rocker Eddy Van Halen named his cat George and his son Wolfgang (poor kid). Legendary newsman Walter Cronkite loved his cat, Dancer. Scott Adams, the creator of the Dilbert comic strip, calls his cats Sarah and Freddy. Bo Derek and Linda Evans have both owned cats named She. The recently deceased and much loved Suzanne Summers HAD called her Chrissy, after her character in Three's Company.

As I have noted, writers love cats. Ernest Hemingway had many, with names like Boise, Crazy Christian, Dillinger, Ecstasy, Friendless Brother, Fur House, and Fats.

F. Scott Fitzgerald had a cat named Chopin. Edgar Allen Poe called his Catarina, Victor Hugo had at least two, which went by the names of Chanoine and Gavroche.

Even cartoon cats are loved by their creators, who see them as family. Felix the Cat was created as a newspaper comic strip drawn by Otto Messmer, and made his first appearance on screen in 1919 in an animated film called Feline Follies. Felix was hugely popular and syndicated in more than 250 newspapers. Charles Lindbergh adopted "Felix the Cat" as his mascot on his famous transatlantic flight. We also can't forget about Garfield, the beloved orange tabby cat that stars in the comic strip created by Jim Davis.

In this modern age, cats have taken over the internet. Cat influencers have been capturing the hearts and minds of people worldwide. These feline celebrities effortlessly dominate social media platforms with their adorable faces and irresistible charm. Some of these whiskered friends have amassed millions of followers online, including Stryker (@strykerthecat on TikTok), Kurt (@abrameng on TikTok), Grumpy Cat (@realgrumpycat on Instagram), and Coby the cat (@cobythecat on Instagram), each with 8.1 million, 6.3 million, 2.4 million, and 1.8 million followers, respectively.

Nala the cat is a pretty famous Siamese and tabby mix. Nala was adopted from a shelter when she was only a kitten, and her owner started an Instagram account for her to share with friends and family. Now, she's an international sensation. Her Instagram account (@nala_cat) has over 4.5 million—yes, million—followers who love the daily posts of this adorable cat.

Beyond the playfulness, adorable personality, and the cutest face you've ever seen, Nala has also become an ambassador for animal rights, animal welfare, and the "adopt-don't-shop" movement. The kitten, who was once surrendered to a shelter after being under-cared for, is now using her vast platform to make a positive impact on the lives of other animals. Nala's rise to stardom serves as a testament to the power of social media in connecting people with these fluffy friends.

The cat is a dilettante in fur.
–THEOPHILE GAUTIER

According to DailyPaws on the web, the most popular names for female cats in 2022 were Luna, Lily, Bella, Lucy, Nala, Callie, Kitty, Cleo, Willow, and Chloe. I feel like I was ahead of the curve on this one, naming my beloved pet Kitty all the way back in the last century… the 1990's! For male cats, the most popular names in 2022 were Oliver, Milo, Leo, Charlie, Max, Loki, Simba, Jack, Ollie, and Jasper.

A cat named Cleo

Chapter 8
The Greatness of Cats: Live Long and Pawsper

MAHATMA GANDHI once said that "the greatness of a nation can be judged by the way its animals are treated." Great minds have explored this idea throughout the ages.

St. Francis of Assisi wrote: "If you have men who will exclude any of God's creatures from the shelter of compassion and pity, you will have men who deal likewise with their fellow men." Albert Schweitzer issued a warning he framed this way: "Anyone who has accustomed himself to regard the life of any living creature as worthless is in danger of arriving at the idea of worthless human lives." And the great American president Abraham Lincoln noted: "I am in favour of animal rights as well as human rights. That is the way of a whole human being."

The domestication of creatures like the cat has given us great comfort, but our pleasure often comes at the expense of the animal's own natural survival instincts and skills. We all recoil in horror at stories of cruelty to animals or abandonment because it highlights how vulnerable our domesticated animals are—they are dependent on us, often for the basics of life.

In any relationship, there must be a sense of commitment and fidelity. But in the case of pets, we must also guard their welfare. It is our responsibility and it is in our own self-interest, but we have much to learn. These creatures can enhance our own humanity; perhaps that is why we can be judged by the way we treat our animals.

The French veterinarian and author Fernand Mery, always erudite on the topic of cats, asks us to ask ourselves this question: "With the qualities of cleanliness, affection, patience, dignity, and courage that cats have, how many of us, I ask you, would be capable of becoming cats?"

It's an interesting question to contemplate. Not many, would be my guess.

> *If we treated everyone we meet with the same affection we bestow upon our favourite cat, they, too, would purr.*
>
> –MARTIN BUXBAUM

I doubt our relationship with cats will, in the end, bring us closer to world peace or bestow eternal harmony on a troubled planet. But there is no doubt in my mind that love for a creature makes each of us a more humane human.

These relationships are intimate and powerful attachments. I recall reading a wonderful line that suggested a good marriage is one in which each partner appoints the other the guardian of his or her solitude. This is precisely the nature of a relationship with a cat. It is time together where words need not be spoken. As the writer Colette once said, "By associating with a cat, one risks only becoming richer."

And now I have a confession to make. Having extolled the virtues of a life in the company of cats, I admit that I LOVED my Kitty best when we WERE apart. It is then that I truly felt the absence of her quiet comfort. I don't mean comfort as in relief from pain or unconditional reassurance that I was always right in my battles with the outside world (Kitty WAS often forced to be an audience of one, listening to my monologues that—after the fact—always offer up the best retorts, rebukes or rebuttals ever given). No, I mean the joy that comes from missing someone or something that needs to be needed. In any relationship, we always feel a healthy tension between getting on with the business of living our daily lives and the guilty tug of abandoning them for too many hours or days. We can placate friends or loved ones with a phone call or a text message. Our ability for direct communication affords us that luxury. But our presence is physically required with our pets—no promise to "do lunch" or send photos will do.

Yes, pets are deep wells into which we throw all our emotions and from which we draw comfort every day.

A Dogs Vs.
A Cat's Diary

Excerpt from a Dog's Diary

Day number 181

8:00 am — Oh boy! Dog food!
My favourite!
9:30 am — Oh boy! A car ride!
My favourite!
9:40 am — Oh boy! A walk!
My favourite!
10:30 am — Oh boy! A car ride!
My favourite!
11:30 am — Oh boy! Dog food!
My favourite!
12:00 noon — Oh boy! The kids!
My favourite!
1:00 pm — Oh boy! The yard!
My favourite!
4:00 pm — Oh boy! The kids!
My favourite!
5:00 pm — Oh boy! Dog food!
My favourite!

Day number 182

8:00 am — Oh boy! Dog food!
My favourite!
9:30 am — Oh boy! A car ride!
My favourite!
9:40 am — Oh boy! A walk!
My favourite!
10:30 am — Oh boy! A car ride!
My favourite!
11:30 am — Oh boy! Dog food!
My favourite!
12:00 noon — Oh boy! The kids!
My favourite!
1:00 pm — Oh boy! The yard!
My favourite!
1:30 pm — Ooooooo. Bath.
Bummer.
4:00 pm — Oh boy! The kids!
My favourite!
5:00 pm — Oh boy! Dog food!
My favourite!

Excerpt from a Cat's Diary

Day number 752

My captors continue to taunt me with bizarre little dangling objects. They dine lavishly on fresh meat, while I am forced to eat dry cereal. The only thing that keeps me from going insane is the hope of escape, and the mild satisfaction I get from ruining the occasional piece of furniture. Tomorrow I may eat another houseplant.

Day number 761

Today my attempt to kill my captors by weaving around their feet while they were walking almost succeeded-must try this at the top of the stairs. In an attempt to disgust and repulse these vile oppressors, I once again induced myself to vomit on their favourite chair...must try this on their bed.

Day number 765

Decapitated a mouse and brought them the headless body, in an attempt to make them aware of what I am capable of and to strike fear into their hearts. They only cooed and condescended about what a good little cat I was... ....Hmmm. Not working according to plan.

Day number 768

I am finally aware of how sadistic they are. For no good reason, I was chosen for the water torture. This time, however, it included a burning foamy chemical called "shampoo." What sick minds could invent such a liquid?My only consolation is the piece of thumb still stuck between my teeth.

Day number 771

There was some sort of gathering of their accomplices. I was placed in solitary throughout the event. However, I could hear the noise and smell the foul odor of the glass tubes they call "beer." More importantly, I overheard that my confinement was due to MY power of "allergies." Must learn what this is and how to use it to my advantage.

Day number 774

I am convinced the other captives are flunkies and maybe snitches. The dog is routinely released and seems more than happy to return. He is obviously a half-wit. The bird, on the other hand, has got to be an informant and speaks with them regularly. I am certain he reports my every move. Due to his current placement in the metal room, his safety is assured.

But I can wait... It is only a matter of time...

Sleepy Cat

Epilogue

I HAD always assumed I was a dog person. I grew up with a beautiful blond cocker spaniel named Bubbles. She was a gentle creature who endlessly tolerated being dressed up and put in a carriage. Yet, she  would have given her life to protect us.

My childhood experience with cats was limited, and my assumptions about them were the usual clichés—to rid the house, the barn, the castle, perhaps even the planet of mice.

As an adult, of course I encountered other people's pets, but the nature of my work and the constant travel meant that for years, I lived a petless life.

But fate then intervened. I reluctantly agreed to kitty-sit for a friend. When she arrived, this tiny chocolate-point Siamese, as delicate and beautiful as anything I had ever seen, she claimed my heart. I didn't want to give her back. Cooler heads prevailed, but my connection with this darling creature was so profound that I began my search for a clone.

Kittens of all kinds were readily available, but not a female, chocolate-point Siamese. Finally, I found a woman who had two "girls." As I came breathlessly through her door, the breeder explained apologetically that she had sold the female. "You said you had two," I countered. She pointed to a corner. A tiny kitten, the abandoned runt of the litter, was huddled there, looking utterly lonely and resigned. I wanted her. And I was not to be deterred. I paid full price, and promised I would make no legal claims if my choice perished. So I carried the precious little creature away in the palm of my hand and toward a future neither she nor I could imagine.

I believe it was Leonardo da Vinci who said that even the smallest feline is a masterpiece, and how true that is! My little Siamese had a brown mask, sable paws, a rich, dark tail, and china-blue eyes. I marvelled at the perfection.

She was at my side through many of the traumas that life offers up—divorce, illness, being fired—and the countless other emotional crises that have punctuated my life story.

A cancer diagnosis meant an uncertain future. In the darkest moments of the night, when the chilling hand of fear gripped my entire body, she stayed close. She seemed to understand what I dared not say aloud.

This phase of our "bonding" taught me a few life lessons. Patience is a virtue. I could depend on her. A cat's purring really does heal human hurts. And being a control freak is not always a good thing. You see, I had no choice but to lie quietly and consider my own character flaws and controlling tendencies—and to finally abandon them in the face of a sweetly demanding feline.

Cats—all cats, big and little—sleep about sixteen hours a day, so she willingly kept me company in bed. And with our new, shared vantage point, I began to see the world differently—through her eyes.

She listened as I talked about my life's regrets and most precious moments. My confessions were for her ears only, and the more I doubted my strength, the closer she drew to me and the quiet comfort she offered helped me rediscover hope.

We moved to New York, where she ruled the town. Several years later she left me, and the loss was inconsolable. You may think me a bit crazy but she still comes to "visit". There are signs. She still listens and hears me. I could have never imagined the true complexity of the bond.

She is the gift that keeps on giving. And now I simply cherish the memories of one of the most powerful relationships that a human and her Kitty can have. She changed me.

Pamela with Kitty

Acknowledgments

Many people are owed thanks for this book.

Anne Bayin is a friend and colleague and, as you will see in these pages, a wonderful photographer.

Sandra MacEachern, whose dogged pursuit of feline facts helped substantiate my own theories and experience.

My thanks as well to Peter Atwood and to Peter Maher for their instinctive understanding of the elegance of the cat.

Rebecca Eckler, a longtime friend, wonderful author, and now a great publisher who loved my book so much, that she decided to give it a second go.

To the executive editors at RE:BOOKS, Emilee Corry and Chloe Robinson. Without you, none of this would have been possible. Thank you.

Copyright Acknowledgements